experience hendrix
THE BEST OF JIMI HENDRIX

ISBN 978-0-7935-9144-2

EXPERIENCE
HENDRIX
"A JIMI HENDRIX FAMILY COMPANY"

EXCLUSIVELY DISTRIBUTED BY

HAL•LEONARD®
CORPORATION
7777 W. BLUEMOUND RD. P.O. BOX 13819 MILWAUKEE, WI 53213

For all works contained herein:
Unauthorized copying, arranging, adapting, recording or public performance is an infringement of copyright.
Infringers are liable under the law.

Visit Hal Leonard Online at
www.halleonard.com

Visit EXPERIENCE HENDRIX Online at
www.jimi-hendrix.com

Purple Haze

Words and Music by Jimi Hendrix

The opening guitar/bass harmony in measures 1 and 2 is known in the realm of music theory as an interval of a tritone (a distance of three whole tones) or a flatted fifth, but to a religious zealot of the Spanish Inquisition it was the fearsome *Diablo in Musica* – the Devil's own musical calling card, forbidden to composers of sacred music by the repressive church of those days. To play it was like ringing Satan's doorbell. It's doubtful that Jimi Hendrix knew of his inspiration's ecclesiastical history, though it is yet another irony in the litany of rock guitar's patron saint – Jimi sure could raise hell when he played.

His choice of notes as well as technique was often unorthodox, but his musical ends always justified the means. A case in point is his use of the thumb for fretting to create unique voicings or free up his other fingers for chord melodies. Note that the G and A major chords in the verse are played in this manner with the thumb fretting the root of each chord.

Jimi also got into electronic effects, most of which were primitive by today's standards, as he searched for new ways to express himself musically. The expertise of Roger Mayer (Jimi's electronics wizard) in this area was a godsend to him and together they came up with many new sounds, creating guitar effects devices that went beyond what was available in the marketplace at that time. The first measure of the guitar solo marks the entrance of a second guitar running through one of Roger's gizmos, the Octavia. This sophisticated distortion unit accentuated the first upper partial of the overtone series, thus creating the octave-doubling heard at this point.

Copyright © 1967, 1980 by EXPERIENCE HENDRIX, L.L.C.
Copyright Renewed 1995
All Rights Controlled and Administered by EXPERIENCE HENDRIX, L.L.C.
All Rights Reserved

3

8

don't know if it's ___ day or night. You got me blow-in',

blow-in' my mind. ___ Is it to - mor - row or just the end of time?

pitch: E

Fire

Words and Music by Jimi Hendrix

The opening octave guitar and bass riff, with its wide open spaces, allows room for drumming ace Mitch Mitchell to stretch out and fill the void in the intro and verses. Guitar and drums come together during the choruses where Jimi shows his masterful way of weaving chords and single-note riffs. The rich and powerful sustained chords in the Bridge section gives way to the Guitar Solo where Jimi layers two nearly identical leads.

Copyright © 1967, 1968, 1980 by EXPERIENCE HENDRIX, L.L.C.
Copyright Renewed 1995, 1996
All Rights Controlled and Administered by EXPERIENCE HENDRIX, L.L.C.
All Rights Reserved

Verse

2. You say your ma-ma ain't home,_ it ain't my con-cern._ Just-a play with me and you won't get burned. I have on-ly one-a itch-in' de-sire,_ *Spoken:* let me stand _ next to your

Yeah! _ Get on with it ba - by!

Guitar Solo

Now, dig this! Ha!

Now lis-ten, ba-by! 3. You try to give me your mon-ey, you bet-ter

24

save it babe, save it for your rain - y day.

I have on - ly one a - burn - in' de - sire, let me stand next to your

The Wind Cries Mary

Words and Music by Jimi Hendrix

This composition will serve as kind of a review of the material already studied concerning Jimi's chordal techniques and will assist you in assimilating his stylistic traits. Throughout the song you will find familiar major chord forms played in conjunction with their related pentatonic scales, often including the fourth of the major scale as well for some brief suspensions. As in "May This Be Love," the suspended fourths occur in conjunction with the tonic chord – in this case F major – and also with the II and IV chords (G and B♭, respectively) during the second half of the guitar solo.

Especially noteworthy is how Hendrix employs the F major pentatonic scale (F, G, A, C, D) against the I-♭VII-IV-♭III progression in the first six measures of the guitar solo. Basically, what he does is only use tones common to this scale and the chord in question. For example, E♭6 is inferred when he plays the G and C doublestop after the third beat in the first measure of the solo and B♭ major ninth via the F major based in the next measure.

Copyright © 1967, 1968, 1980 by EXPERIENCE HENDRIX, L.L.C.
Copyright Renewed 1995, 1996
All Rights Controlled and Administered by EXPERIENCE HENDRIX, L.L.C.
All Rights Reserved

Verse
Moderately Slow Rock ♩ = 78

1. Af - ter all the jacks __ are in their box - es, and the clowns have all __ gone to bed, __ you can hear hap-pi-ness stag-ger-in' __ on down the street, __

*T – Thumb on ⑥

let ring

3. The traf-fic lights, they turn, uh, blue to-mor-row,___ and

shine their emp-ti-ness down on my bed. The ti-ny is-land sags down-stream 'cause the life that lived is, is dead. And the

Hey Joe

Words and Music by Billy Roberts

"Hey Joe" is the only cover tune on *Are You Experienced?* and, ironically, the most requested "signature piece" through-out Jimi's career. According to Hendrix, the tune's popularity gave him sufficient airplay to be asked to play the Monterey Pop Festival in June of 1967 and return triumphantly to the States. Though it was written by someone else, JImi's treatment of the guitar pyrotechnics and the tune's arrangement made it totally his own. The song provided a perfect vehicle for Jimi's choral style by virtue of its "back-cycling" progression of IV-I-V-II-VI. As in "Purple Haze," there is fretting with the thumb, this time to retain the roots of the chords as he plays fills. In the solo, the E minor pentatonic scale (E, G, A, B, D) is used throughout — until he "walks" in unison with the bass in a chromatic fashion through the changes. The guitar sound is clean and the only noticeable effect is a bit of reverb, although that may be actually the result of ambient miking in a "live" room.

© 1962 (Renewed) by THIRD STORY MUSIC, INC.
All Rights Reserved   International Copyright Secured

too cool.
)

2. Uh, hey, ___ Joe, ___

I heard you ___ shot your

wom-an down, ___ you shot her down, now. _____

mess-in' 'round town. _

Uh, yes I did, I shot her, you know I caught my old la-dy mess-in' 'round

Ah.

48

Shoot her one more time a - gain, __ ba - by! Ooh. ____

Hey, Joe! Yeah!

52

way down _____ to Mex-i-co _____ way!
Joe!

Al - right! ___
Hey, _____

I'm go-in' way down south, _

he ain't gon-na put a rope a-round me! You bet-ter be-lieve ___ it right ___ now! ___ I got-ta go ___ now!

Joe, where you gon - na go?

Begin Fade

N.C.(C) (G) (D) (A)

Hey, ___ hey, hey, ___ Joe,

Hey, ___ Joe, you bet - ter run ___ on ___ down! where you gon - na

All Along the Watchtower

Words and Music by Bob Dylan

Bob Dylan liked Jimi's version of his song "All Along the Watchtower" so much that he used the same arrangement when he re-recorded it. The chord progression: C#m - B - A - B is based on the C# Aeolian mode or natural minor scale (C#, D#, E, F#, G#, A, B). Next to the familiar 12-bar blues, the i - bVII - bVI progression is probably the most widely-used progression in contemporary rock music. The rhythm track consists of an acoustic 12-string guitar played by Dave Mason, who at that time was a member of Traffic.

This song's outstanding feature is a highly structured second Guitar Solo section that breaks down into four eight-measure segments of contrasting moods. The first segment is very similar to the opening lead and is based primarily on the C# minor pentatonic scale (C#, E, F#, G#, B). The exception is when he plays D#, the second degree of the C# Aeolian mode, in the last two measures by bending C# up a whole tone. He follows up all that aggressive blues-tinged soloing with some mellow slide-work on an electric 12-string. The generous application of tape echo to this track, creates the illusion of additional guitars playing counter melodies and harmonies. The third segment is on a 6-string electric through a wah-wah pedal and commences with ascending octaves *a la* Wes Montgomery. Jimi then goes into a chordal interlude that uses dominant seventh and add nine substitutions for six measures, then climaxes this final segment with a series of ascending unison bends.

The C# minor pentatonic is used for many of the verse fills, the only exceptions are in the second measure of this repeated progression. An A major chord occurs at that point so the A major pentatonic (A, B, C#, E, F#) is often used, as in measures 11 and 13, for example.

Copyright © 1968 (Renewed), 1985 Dwarf Music
International Copyright Secured   All Rights Reserved
Reprinted by Permission of Music Sales Corporation

1. There must be some kind a way

But uh,   but you   and I, we've   been __ through that,   but, ah,   and this   is   not our   fate.__

So let   us not   talk   false - ly now,   the ho - ur's get - tin' __ late, __

* Played ahead of the beat.

64

3. Well,

all a - long __ the watch - tow-er, prin-ces kept the view. __

70

Two rid-ers were ap-proach-in' _____ and the wind be-gan to howl. Hey! Ah.

74

Well, all a - long the watch - tow -

- er.

Fade Out

Stone Free

Words and Music by Jimi Hendrix

Jimi was a complex individual who, above all else, wanted to live a life filled with the simplicity that only total freedom could provide. The lyrics to this song convey the gypsy element of his persona. For instance, he states, "I don't want to be tied down" and "I gotta move before I get caught," which aptly describes the spirit of his lifestyle and all his creative pursuits. As far as the latter goes, he was constantly searching for new ways to express himself and didn't want to paint himself into a corner, musically speaking, or find himself in a "plastic cage."

Compositionally, Hendrix would often use progressions as a starting point for a song's harmonic scheme. In "Stone Free," the verse section is a variation on the i-iv-i-iv progression of the first eight measures of a twelve-bar blues. A temporary modulation occurs at the chorus from the key of E minor to D major to unleash Jimi, the explorer, upon new harmonic territories.

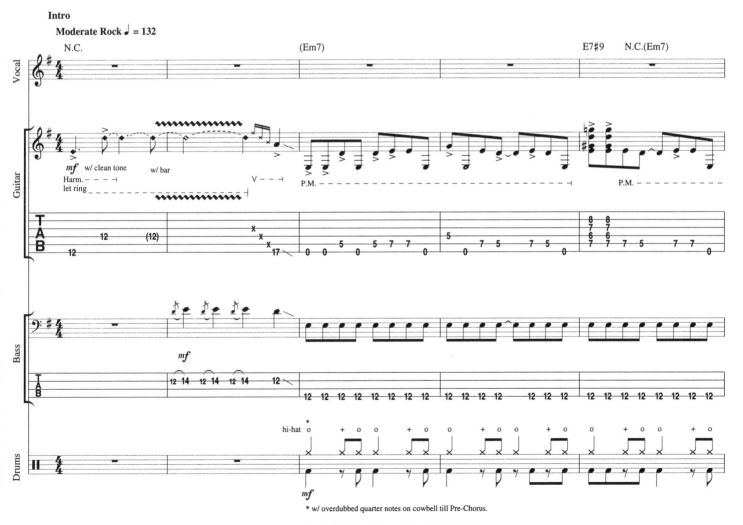

* w/ overdubbed quarter notes on cowbell till Pre-Chorus.

Copyright © 1966 by PALL MALL MUSIC LTD.
Copyright Renewed 1994
All Rights Controlled and Administered by EXPERIENCE HENDRIX, L.L.C.
All Rights Reserved

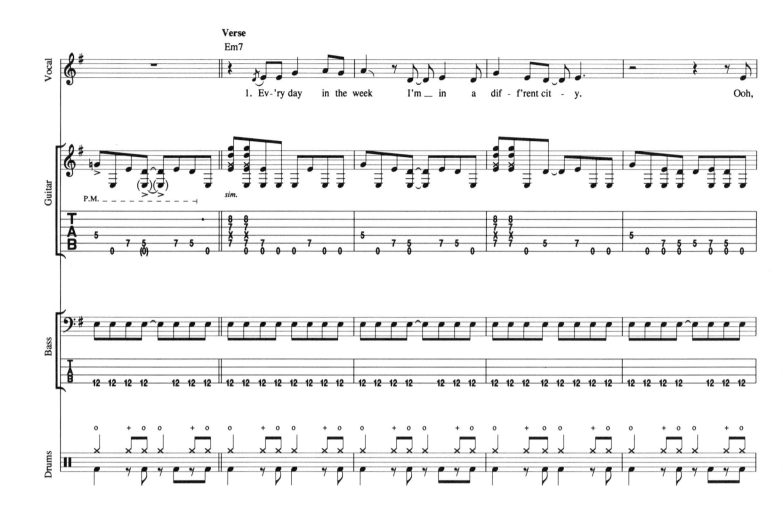

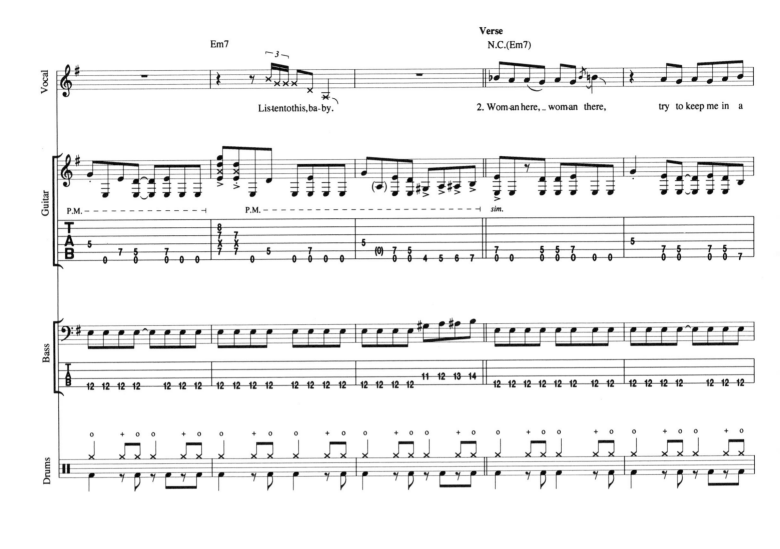

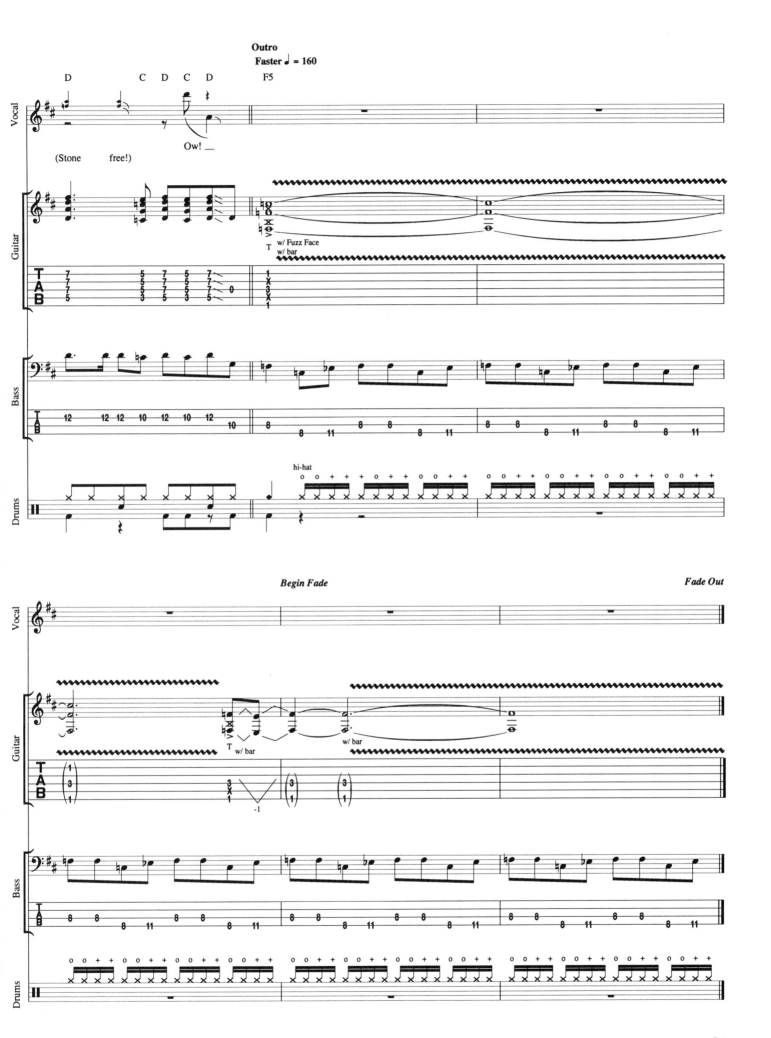

Crosstown Traffic

Words and Music by Jimi Hendrix

Jimi used the scat-singing style of early jazz singers in unison with the guitar for the opening riff to this song, a device that was later popularized by George Benson. The basic chord progression in the first verse (C#7 - F#7, followed by a turnaround of Bm7 - E7 - Am7 - G#7) is jazz-related and includes a series of harmonies where the first three chords of the turnaround move in ascending fourths. Such harmonic sophistication was practically unheard-of in rock at that time. In the second verse he even goes beyond the confines of the basic progression and throws in some altered dominant chords. Instead of playing a C#7 Jimi usually opts for C#7#9, whose inherent major/minor ambiguity is the result of a raised ninth being enharmonic to the flatted third of a major chord.

Mitch Mitchell's jazz background is noticeable even in the little rhythmic twists he comes up with. He often intersperses short, sometimes syncopated, 16th-note fills within the standard 4/4 rock beat. A good example of this is at the end of the intro in measures 9 and 10.

The only two scales used in this song are the G# minor pentatonic scale (G#, B, C#, D#, F#), for the guitar solo, and the C# blues scale (C#, E, F#, G, G#, B), for the main riff and outro fills.

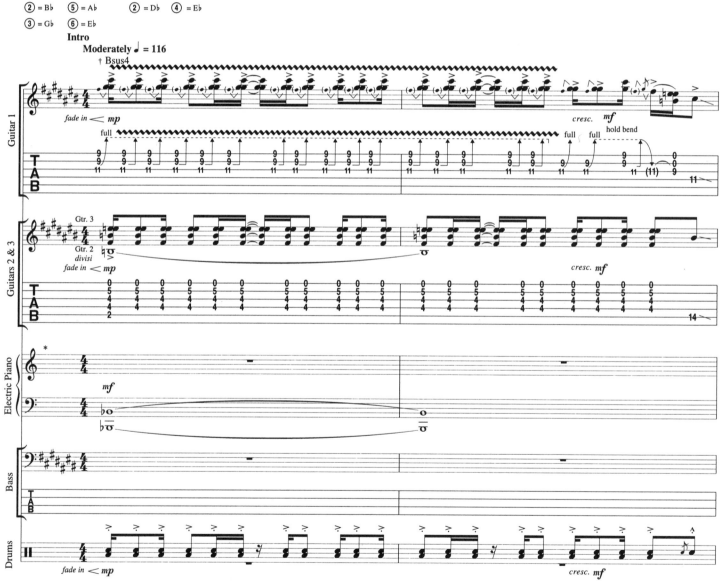

† Chord symbols represent implied tonality.

* The piano part is written in actual sounding pitch whereas the guitar, bass and vocal notation
  along with the chord symbols reflect the guitars and bass being detuned 1/2 step.

Copyright © 1968 by EXPERIENCE HENDRIX, L.L.C.
Copyright Renewed 1996
All Rights Controlled and Administered by EXPERIENCE HENDRIX, L.L.C.
All Rights Reserved

Do, do, do, do, do, do, do, do, do, do.

You tell me it's al - right, _ a-heh, you don't mind a lit - tle pain, _____ ah.

You say you just want me to take you for a drive. _____

slow me down, ___ and I'm try-in' to get on the oth - er side of town.
Do, do, do, ___ do, do, do.
Do,do, do,do, do, do, ___ do,do, do, do.)

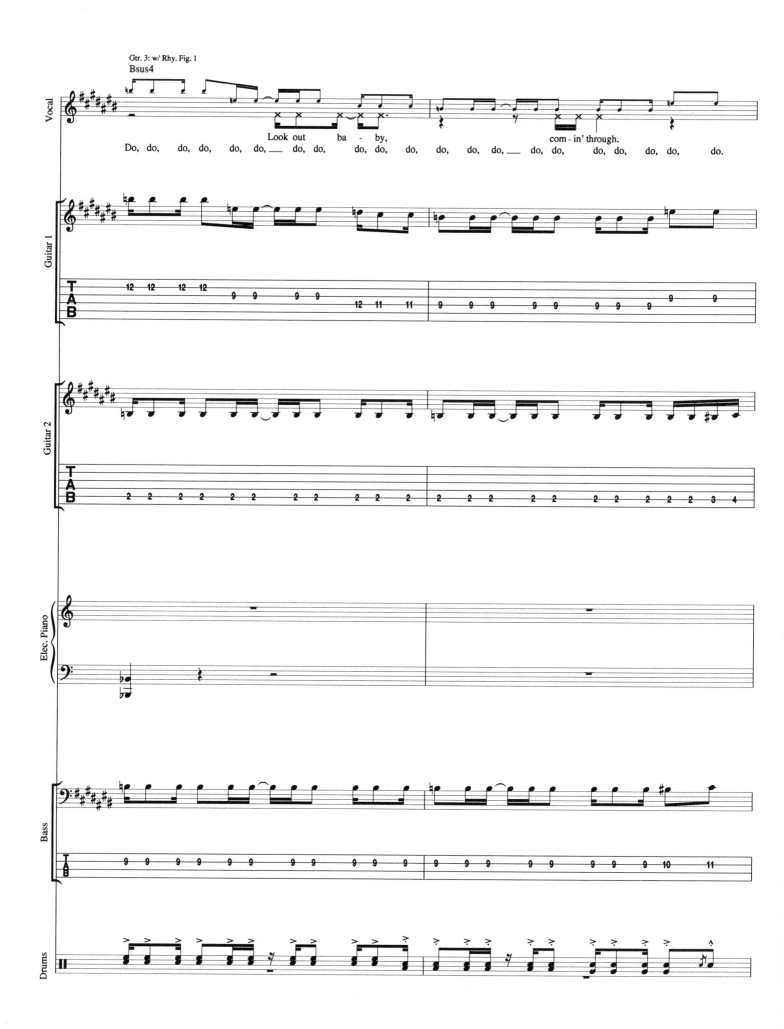

Gtr. 3: w/ Rhy. Fig. 1

Look out ba - by, com - in' through.

Do, do, do, do, do, do, do, do, do, do, do, do, do, do, do, do, do, do, do, do. do.

Begin Fade

Bsus4

Look out,_____ look out_____ ba - by.

Do, do, do, do, do, do,___ do, do, do, do, do, do, do, do,___ do, doo-dle,___ do, do, do.

Fade Out

Manic Depression

Words and Music by Jimi Hendrix

You'll notice that the time signature for this ode to mental anguish is 3/4, a meter division most musicians associate with the generic waltzes you might hear when at a skating rink. Well, that was before Jimi and his Experience made it swing like the pendulum moods of a manic depressive.

This composition and "Fire" showcase the talents of drummer Mitch Mitchell, giving him a chance to display his chops as he propels Hendrix' Strat to new heights, especially during the interlude. In this section, the first eight measures consist of unison bends that climb up the harmonic extensions of A minor, commencing with the fifth and sequentially ascending to the eleventh. From there, with the use of large interval bends, notes on the verge of feedback, and wide vibrato with the whammy bar, Jimi creates an aural metaphor of a mind's journey into psychosis.

For the most part, Jimi's solo is based on the A minor pentatonic scale (A, C, D, E, G); the only deviations are in measures 18 and 20, where he bends up to F♮, the major 6th. The feedback has been notated throughout, though you may have a bit of difficulty in recreating it. One sure-fire way of generating feedback corresponding to any pitch played is to pick the note and place the guitar neck against the speaker cabinet. This technique is apparently employed in the eighteenth through twenty-fourth measures of the guitar solo.

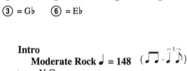

* Key signature denotes A Mixolydian.

Copyright © 1967, 1968 by EXPERIENCE HENDRIX, L.L.C.
Copyright Renewed 1995, 1996
All Rights Controlled and Administered by EXPERIENCE HENDRIX, L.L.C.
All Rights Reserved

116

pres-sion is a catch-in' my soul. _____ Yeah. _____

Verse

2. Wom-an so wear-y, the sweet cause in

Guitar Solo

N.C.(A7)

* C note (3rd str., 17 fr.) is bent with 3rd finger, which also catches G (4th str., 17 fr.) bending it approx. 1 step. This pitch is sounded by "feeding-back" and is not picked.

** D note (5th str., 17 fr.) is also caught w/ 3rd finger (G, D and A strs. are all fretted, with 3rd finger). As the bend on the G str. is released, the D str. is bent approx. 1/2 step.

Outro

Mu - sic, sweet mu - sic, sweet mu - sic, sweet mu - sic, ah!

Mu - sic, sweet mu - sic, sweet mu - sic. Yeah!

Little Wing

Words and Music by Jimi Hendrix

Jimi's protean imagination is evident in his unique chordal style, particularly in a ballad like "Little Wing." In this context, his approach to the guitar is more like that of a pianist: Jimi breaks away from the confines of the dogmatic "rhythm or lead" method. His thumb frets the bass notes, functioning in almost the same manner as a keyboardist's left hand, and the fingers of his fretting hand can be likened to a pianist's right hand. Let's examine a few excerpts that demonstrate this piano style format and rediscover what Adrian Belew has called a "lost art."

On the first beat of measure 2, Jimi frets the root of the G major chord with his thumb, allowing it to be sustained as he follows up with the chord melody. Although the melody is within the third position form of G major, the complete chord is not fingered at any one time. Jimi usually plays dyads (double stops) and movement within these partial chords is oblique; that is one pitch is stationary. If you examine measure 6 you'll find extensive use of oblique motion.

Going to the second verse, an example of parallel motion can be found in measure 2, as the interval of a fourth is slid back and forth over a distance of a whole tone. This idea based on the major pentatonic scale also appears in the coda to "The Wind Cries Mary."

The unusual tonal quality of Jimi's guitar is characteristic of the pickup combination known as the "out-of-phase" mode (positions 2 & 4 of a 5 position pickup selector switch). The ethereal effect beginning with measure 6 is the result of playing through a unit associated with organists, the rotating speaker cabinet or "Leslie." Actually, it's the speaker baffle that moves, creating slow or fast vibration on the principle of the Doppler effect.

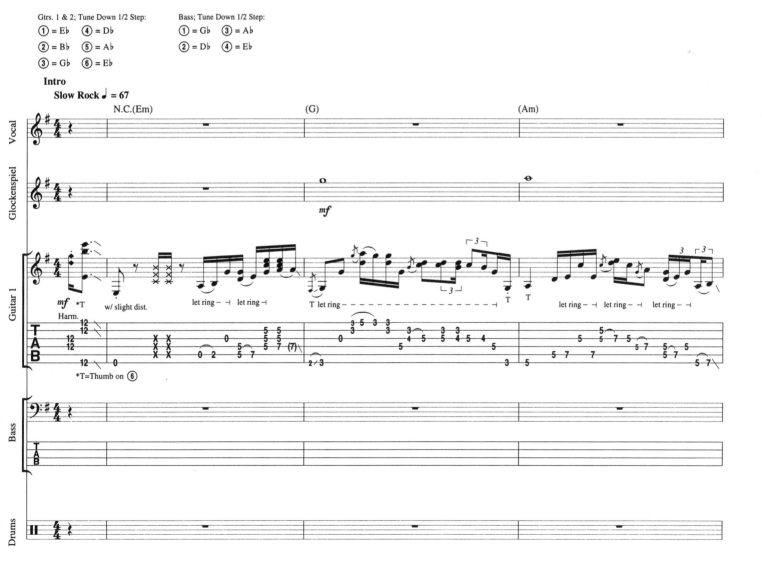

Copyright © 1968, 1977 by EXPERIENCE HENDRIX, L.L.C.
Copyright Renewed 1996
All Rights Controlled and Administered by EXPERIENCE HENDRIX, L.L.C.
All Rights Reserved

Fade Out

lit-tle ba - by. _

142

If 6 Was 9

Words and Music by Jimi Hendrix

One outstanding feature of this song is that during the verses Jimi doubles his vocal line with the guitar. This device was first used, but to a much lesser extent, in the guitar solo to "Manic Depression" from *Are You Experienced?* There, it was done in unison instead of an octave below his voice, as found here.

Moving along to the bridge, the format switches to chordal accomplishment and the song's momentum builds. Jimi's penchant for lush, complex voicings is evident as he opts to use ninth chords for the first three chords in this descending progression. From a theoretical standpoint, this form naturally occurs when harmonizing on the dominant or fifth degree of a major scale. For example, if we took the D major scale (D E F♯ G A B C♯) and began constructing a chord on A, the fifth degree, by superimposing intervals of a third (tertian harmony), our first true chord would be a major triad consisting of A, C♯ and E. Continuing in the same manner will result in various harmonic extensions (7, 9, 11 and 13), but for our purposes we'll just require the seventh, G, and then replace the third, C♯, with the second, B, to form the ninth.

Copyright © 1968, 1977 by EXPERIENCE HENDRIX, L.L.C.
Copyright Renewed 1996
All Rights Controlled and Administered by EXPERIENCE HENDRIX, L.L.C.
All Rights Reserved

148

Interlude

Spoken: White col-lar con-ser-va-tive flash-in' down the street point-in' their plas-tic fin-ger at me, ha.

They're hop-in' that soon my kind will drop and die, _ but, uh, I'm ___ gon-na wave my free flag high, _

*Drum Solo

*w/ voc. ad Lib (next 12 meas.)

158

160

Foxey Lady

Words and Music by Jimi Hendrix

The introduction is the most difficult section of this song to replicate, but not impossible, especially if sufficient "woodshedding" has been devoted to feedback techniques outlined in preceding selections. Here's how it's done: the F♯ is shaken in exaggerated wide vibrato, so much that the adjacent strings sound as indicated, while the volume is kept low on the guitar. As you bring up the gain, the regenerative cycle of feedback should commence, its crescendo followed by a slide into the F♯m7 rhythm figure. This brief segment is a superb example of Jimi's innovative use of guitaristic "noises" to create imagery, in this case, his own rising passion. The incredible version of "Star Spangled Banner" he performed at Woodstock is incomparable in regard to its sonic portrayal of war.

The guitar solo is primarily based on the F♯ minor pentatonic scale (F♯, A, B, C♯, E) except for the inclusion of the ninth (G♯) in the third and sixth measures as in "Manic Depression."

† Key signature denotes F♯ Dorian.

Copyright © 1967, 1968, 1980 by EXPERIENCE HENDRIX, L.L.C.
Copyright Renewed 1995, 1996
All Rights Controlled and Administered by EXPERIENCE HENDRIX, L.L.C.
All Rights Reserved

Bold as Love

Words and Music by Jimi Hendrix

The flower of Jimi's lyrical genius is in full bloom throughout *Axis: Bold As Love*, especially the title cut, with its imagery and personification of the colors. "Lyrical" is also an apt adjective for his guitar playing, whether it be the chordal counterpoint within the verses or the lead lines during the majestic outro solo.

Examining the guitar solo from a theoretical standpoint will reveal why it works in relationship to the chord progression and should help you in developing your own melodies. For example, the solo commences on the root of the A major chord in the form of a string bend, then it moves along to roots of the next two chords in the progression, E major and F# minor. In the third and fifth measures he bends to C#, which is the third of the A major triad (A C# E), then releases it back to B, the fifth of the E major triad (E G# B).

Following this section, Mitch plays a brief solo interlude wherein his drums are colored by ace engineer Eddie Kramer with a bit of studio magic known as flanging. Current state-of-the-art technology makes this effect available electronically, but when *Axis: Bold As Love* was produced it was done mechanically. This required manipulating the reel flange (projecting rim) to one of two tape decks running simultaneously, with the thumb and mixing the resulting signal.

The music of the majestic grand finale seems to take flight and "kiss the sky" on its new course of C# major. Note that beginning with the measure 11, Jimi uses arpeggios based on the C# - G# - A#M - B - B# progression, and fades out with tremolo picked partial chords.

Copyright © 1968, 1977, 1980 by EXPERIENCE HENDRIX, L.L.C.
Copyright Renewed 1996
All Rights Controlled and Administered by EXPERIENCE HENDRIX, L.L.C.
All Rights Reserved

Jeal-ous-y, en-vy waits _ be-hind him, her fire-y green _ gown _ sneers at the grass-y ground. ___

Blue are the life giv-ing wa - ters tak-ing for grant-ed, they qui-et-ly un-der-stand. ___

w/ clean tone

* Doubles bass gtr. simile at this point.

182

Once hap - py tur-quoise arm - ies lay op-po-site, read - y, but won-der why the fight is on. _____

Yeah,   they're all _____ bold   as   love, _____   yeah!

Or - ange is young, __ full of dar-ing, but ver - y un - stead-y for the first go round. __

My Yel-low in this case _ is not so mel-low. In fact, I'm try'n' to say it's fright-ened like me. _

And all of these e-mo-tions of mine keeps hold-ing me from, uh, giv-ing my life to a rain-bow like you. But I'm, uh,

194

Outro Solo

Gtr. 1 tacet

* Chords played to Mellotron (early kybd. sampler that utilized tapes vs. electronics) for remainder of tune.

* 2nd string sounds unintentionally.

198

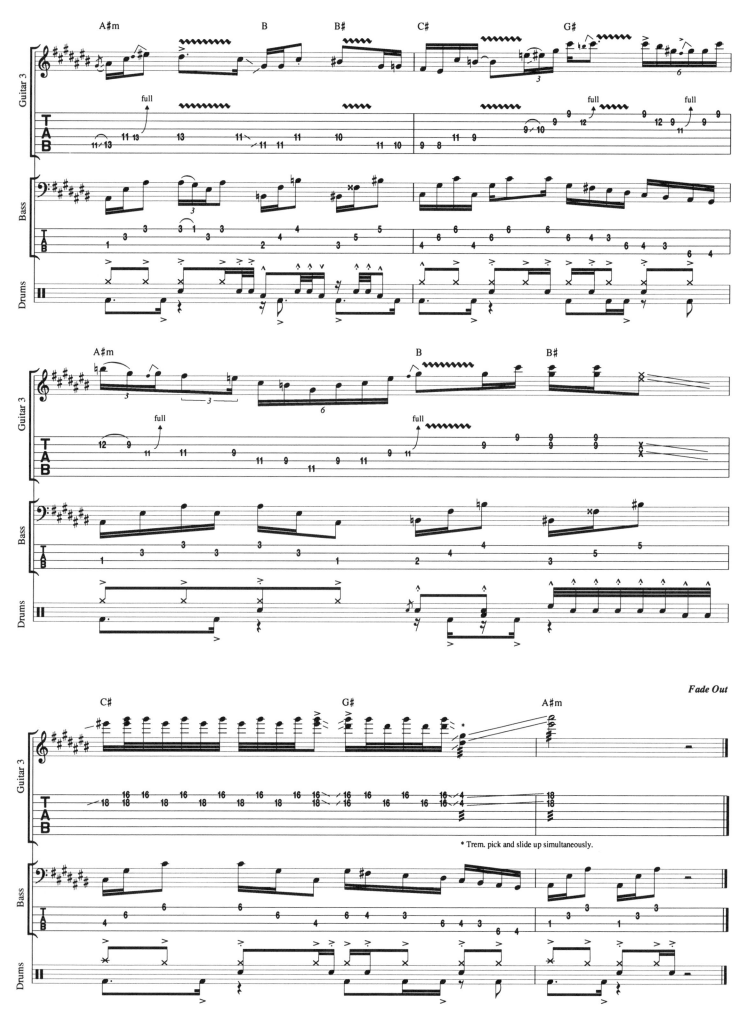

* Trem. pick and slide up simultaneously.

Fade Out

Castles Made of Sand

Words and Music by Jimi Hendrix

Whereas Jimi's anthem to nonconformity, "If 6 Was 9," was vehemently subjective in its declarations, here he is more or less a detached observer of life's ironies. There's even a certain pathos to the music itself which can be attributed to the fact that there are brief departures from the major mode to minor.

The first voicing, G5add 9 (also called Gsus2) has a rather bittersweet quality to it, being neither "fish nor fowl" (i.e. major nor minor), and then B♭, the minor third, is introduced by virtue of the parallel movement of the opening chordal figure and its recapitulation at the song's conclusion. Note also that the minor mode is inferred by the entrance of a B♭ major chord in the last measures of the introduction.

As in "You Got Me Floating," there's that ubiquitous "backwards" guitar in the background, and this time it is also the solo instrument.

Memorization of this song is a must for any guitar-playing Hendrix devotee. Just ask Frank Marino of Mahogany Rush fame, an "honor student" of the Jimi Hendrix school of guitar.

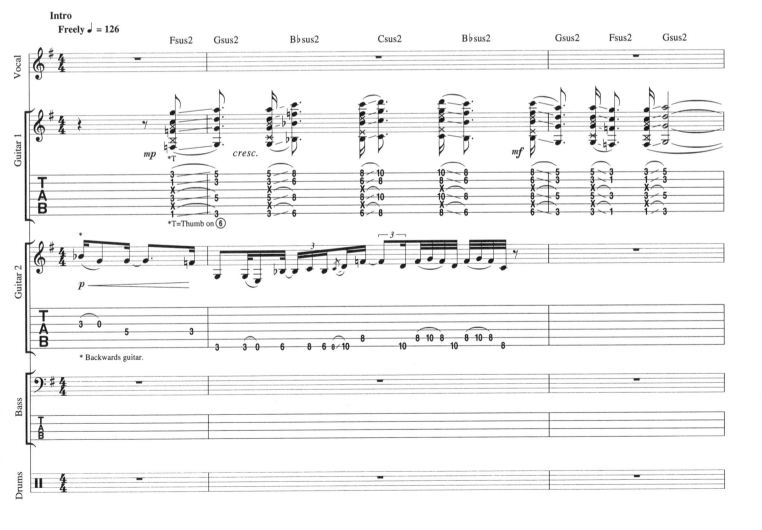

Copyright © 1968, 1977 by EXPERIENCE HENDRIX, L.L.C.
Copyright Renewed 1996
All Rights Controlled and Administered by EXPERIENCE HENDRIX, L.L.C.
All Rights Reserved

1. Down the street you can hear her scream, "You're a dis - grace," as she

* Vibrato G intermittently "bumps into" C note, 3rd str., 5th fret.

Verse

was a young girl whose heart was a frown. 'cause she was crip-pled for life and she could-n't speak a sound. And she

wished and prayed she could stop liv-in', so she de - cid-ed to die.

212

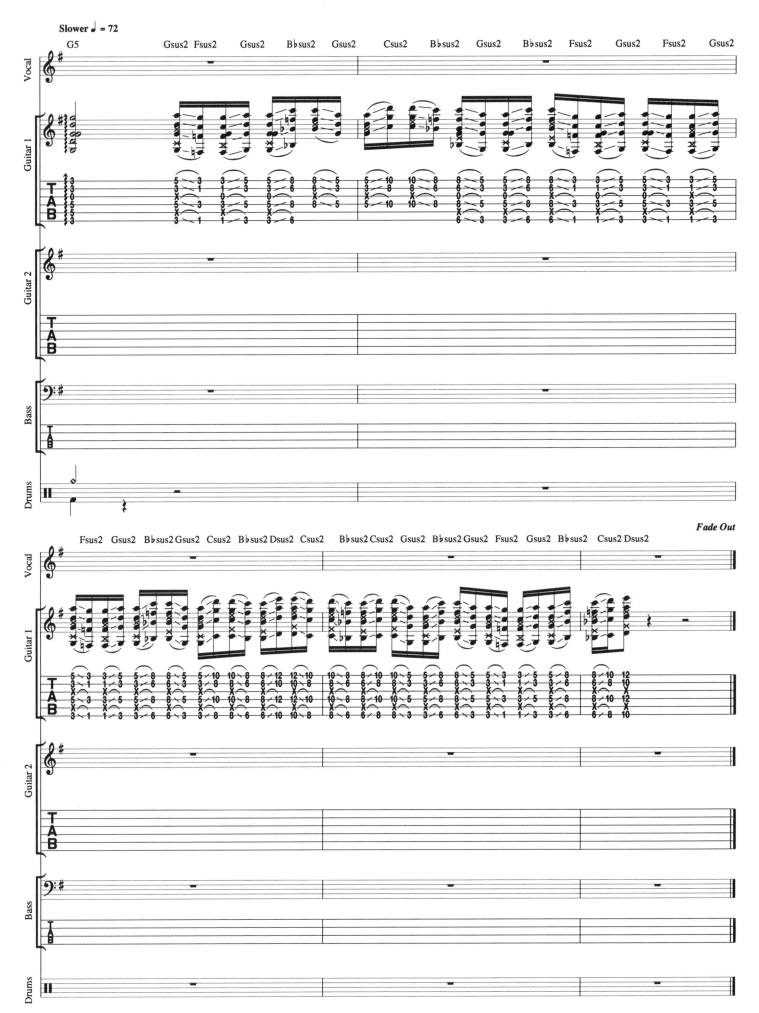

Red House

Words and Music by Jimi Hendrix

What sounds like a bass on this recording is actually Noel Redding playing a hollowbody electric six string guitar with the bass tones boosted via the guitar's tone control. (Noel was strictly a guitarist before joining the Experience.)

Jimi draws on various scales for different shades of "blue." For example, the melancholy fill in measure 20 is based on the B blues scale (B, D, E, F, F#, A) and the warmer, more "down home" lick he follows it with three measures later is based on the B major pentatonic (B, C#, D#, F#, G#). Other fingerings for the latter scale occur throughout, as in the run back in measure 8 that shifts from the 9th to the 12th position by way of a slurred slide with the ring finger. This last pattern is a favorite of B.B. King's.

Learning these scales is certainly a good starting place for the aspiring blues guitarist, but they tell only part of the musical story. One possibility is to use chord tones in conjunction with these scales and throw in some double-stops and complete chords every now and then. Hendrix demonstrates this approach very tastefully in measures 33 and 34 with a series of major sixths.

Copyright © 1967, 1968, 1980 by EXPERIENCE HENDRIX, L.L.C.
Copyright Renewed 1995, 1996
All Rights Controlled and Administered by EXPERIENCE HENDRIX, L.L.C.
All Rights Reserved

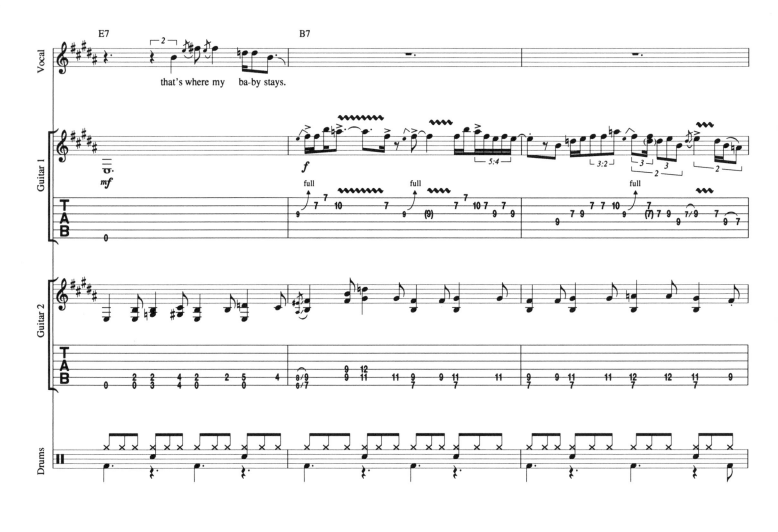

Ain't_ been home to see my_ ba-by   in 'bout nine-ty nine and one half years._

2. Wait a min-ute, some-thing's wrong here,_

Spoken: Some-thing's go-in' wrong here.

door.

I have a bad, _

_ bad _ feel-in', uh, _

that my ba-by

don't live here no more.

Guitar Solo

Spoken: That's al-right, I still got my gui-tar. Look out, now! _ Yeah! _

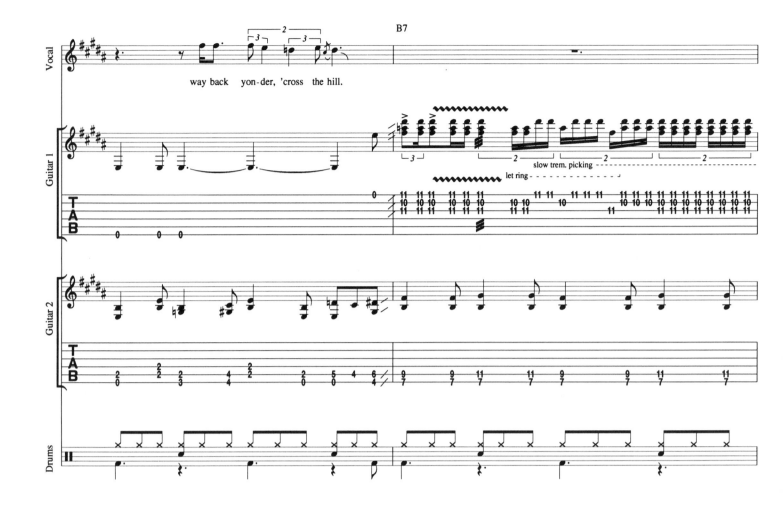

way back yon-der, 'cross the hill.

Voodoo Child (Slight Return)

Words and Music by Jimi Hendrix

Right after "Voodoo Chile" was recorded, a camera crew came into the studio and this second version was then played, thus providing them with something to film.

The intro consists of some nice interplay between Jimi's wah-wahed Stratocaster and Mitch Mitchell's drums. Then, in measure 13, Noel Redding enters on bass for a 12-measure vamp that sets the mood for this harder edged version. During the verses Jimi's vocal is again doubled by his guitar and he returns to the vamp between the lines.

In measures 16 and 17 he flicks the pickup selector switch while releasing the bend. This move and also some of his vibrato bar antics were often done with his left arm as the controls were on top and within reach of it since he played right-hand guitars in a reversed fashion. In this manner he was able to do these same moves while picking.

The E minor pentatonic scale (E, G, A, B, D) is primarily used for the guitar solos, but often he'll throw in a G♯, the major third, which is common in blues due to its major/minor ambiguity. Many of the other notes that occur outside of this scale are the result of intentionally overbending a particular note *a la* Albert King, for example, the C note at the end of measure 53 and the B♭ in measure 56.

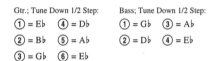

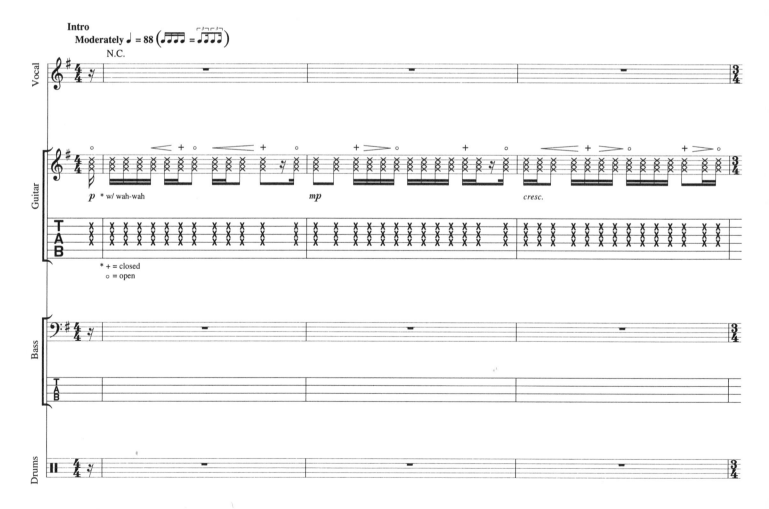

Copyright © 1968 by EXPERIENCE HENDRIX, L.L.C.
Copyright Renewed 1996
All Rights Controlled and Administered by EXPERIENCE HENDRIX, L.L.C.
All Rights Reserved

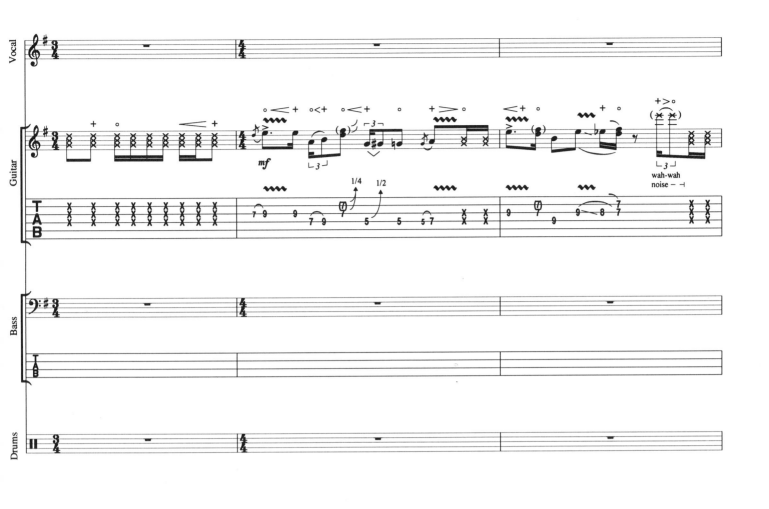

** This harmonic occurs often in the
arrangement in conjunction with the E note,
& is produced either as an P.H. from the E
itself, or is a natural harmonic produced
by the sympathetic vibration of the B string.

* Chord symbols reflect overall tonality.

232

* Flick pickup selector between
neck (N) and middle (M) pickups
in specified rhythm.

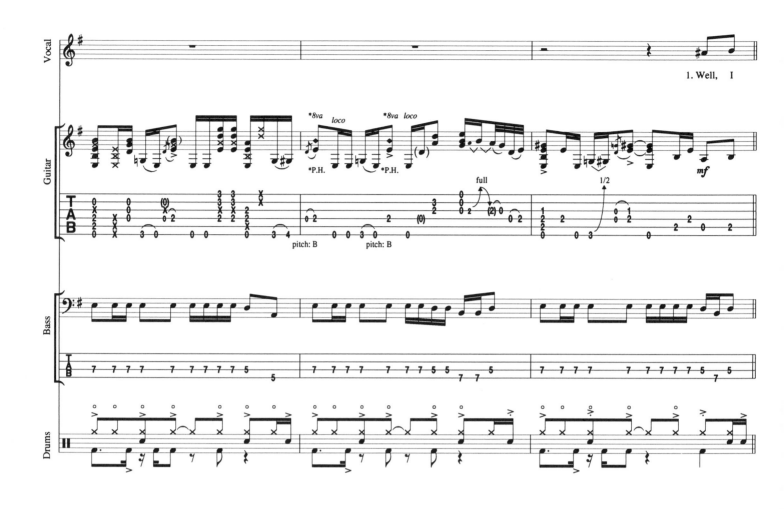

hand. _   Well, I   pick up all the pie - ces and make an is - land, _

might ev - en   raise a _ lit - tle sand. _   Yeah, _   'cause I'm   a

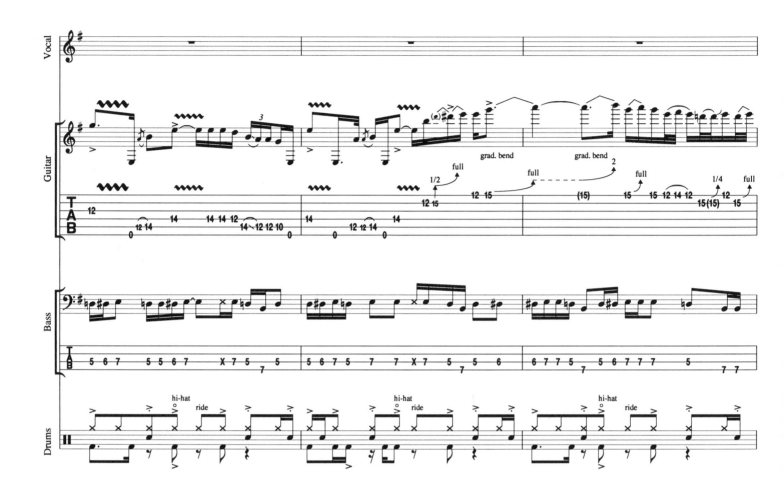

239

I wan-na say one more last thing.

240

Outro Guitar Solo

* Flick pickup selector
  between neck (N) and
  bridge (B) pickups in
  specified rhythm.

Freedom

Words and Music by Jimi Hendrix

Originally released in 1971 on *The Cry of Love* album and re-released in 1997 on *First Rays of the New Rising Sun*, this song is rooted in funk and R&B. As in "Purple Haze," and "Stone Free," (just to name a few) Jimi employs his favorite altered chord, his signature 7#9 chord. "Freedom" begins in the key of C# minor, where it remains until the Bridge section. Here the song changes to the key of F# minor where, it remains throughout the Guitar Solo. Notice how Jimi changes his guitar sound in the thirteenth through sixteenth measures of the solo by rolling back the tone control on his Strat. After the Guitar Solo, the song once again returns to its original key.

Copyright © 1971 by EXPERIENCE HENDRIX, L.L.C.
All Rights Controlled and Administered by EXPERIENCE HENDRIX, L.L.C.
All Rights Reserved

1. You got my _ pride hang-in' out-ta my bed. You mess-in' with my

* Fade in w/ volume pedal or knob.

stick in your dag-ger 'n some-one else so I can leave. Set me free!

* Chord symbols reflect overall tonality.

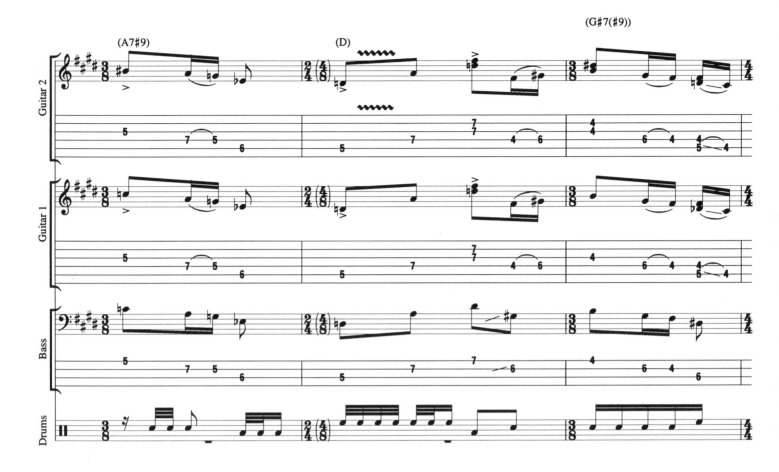

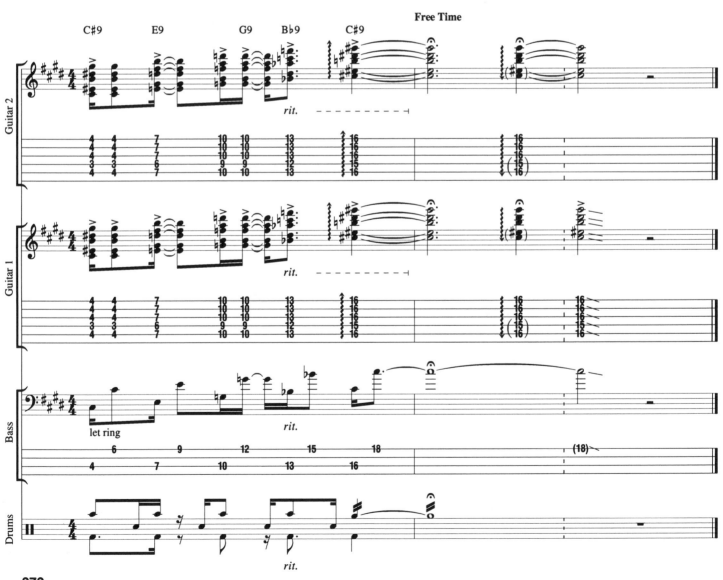

Night Bird Flying

Words and Music by Jimi Hendrix

A notable feature of "Night Bird Flying" is Jimi's use of twin guitar leads, played an octave apart, which enter in the fifth measure of the intro and appear again in the second verse. During the Guitar Solo, guitars 1 and 2 play a series of recurring riffs an octave apart, which is doubled by the bass an octave below. The multiple layered harmony guitars, coupled with a slide guitar, the extended lead solos, and the fact that this song is in the key of E major, all give this song a Southern Rock flavor.

Copyright © 1971, 1996 by EXPERIENCE HENDRIX, L.L.C.
All Rights Controlled and Administered by EXPERIENCE HENDRIX, L.L.C.
All Rights Reserved

Guitar Interlude

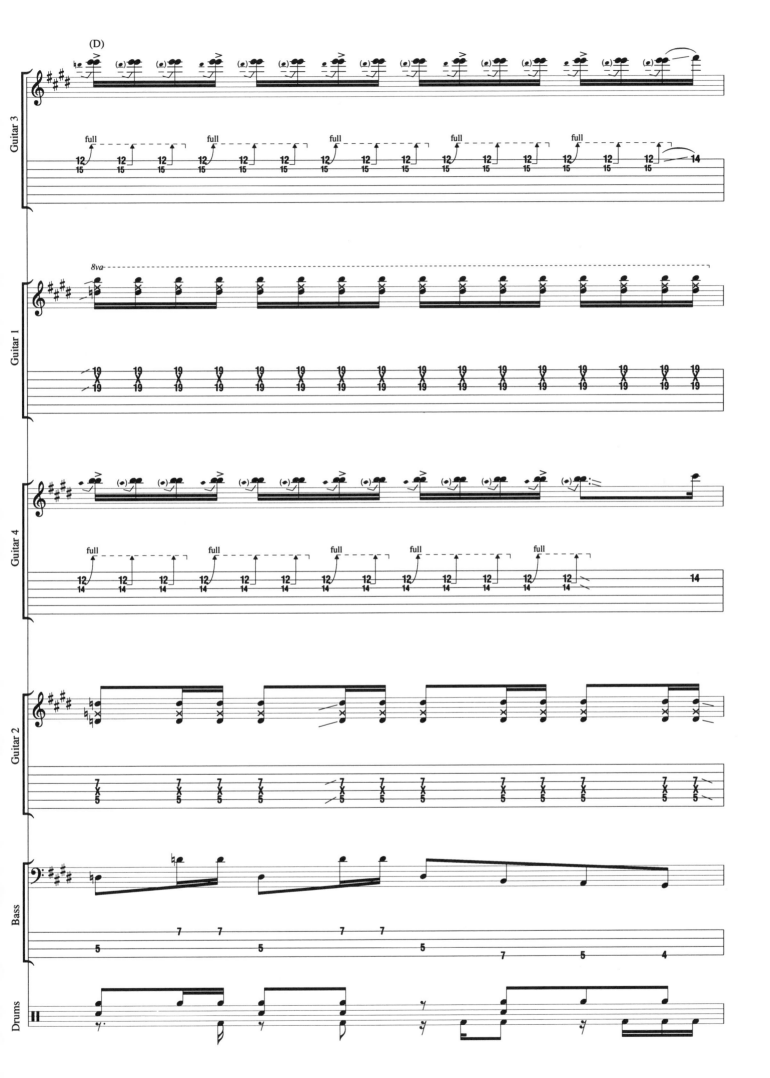

307

Outro

Gtr. 3 tacet

312

Angel

Words and Music by Jimi Hendrix

Written in early 1968 and inspired by a dream about his mother, Lucille, "Angel" is another of Jimi's songs that speaks of being "saved" by a benevolent visitor from a far-off land. "Angel came down from heaven yesterday, she stayed with me just long enough to rescue me," Jimi sings in the first line of the first verse. Jimi spoke of similar visitation/rescues in the songs "Hey Baby (New Rising Sun)," "Long Hot Summer Night" and in "In From The Storm."

Jimi begins the song with full and partial arpeggiations of beautiful (and unusual) chord voicings of Emaj9 and A6/E, as played in measures 1 through 4 of the intro. Both voicings make effective use of the open high E string. The Emaj9 voicing can be analyzed as a second inversion (fifth in the bass) G#m7 chord voicing played over an E pedal, resulting in an overall harmony of Emaj9. The A6/E voicing is the exact same chord form, moved down two frets. This chord can be analyzed as a second inversion F#m7 voicing played over an E pedal, resulting in an overall harmony of A6/E. This same form (without the note on the A string) is moved high up the neck in measure 3 for the Aadd9 and Bmaj11 chords. This chordal work is yet another example of Jimi Hendrix's genius and inventiveness as a rhythm guitarist *par excellence*.

Copyright © 1972 by EXPERIENCE HENDRIX, L.L.C.
All Rights Controlled and Administered by EXPERIENCE HENDRIX, L.L.C.
All Rights Reserved

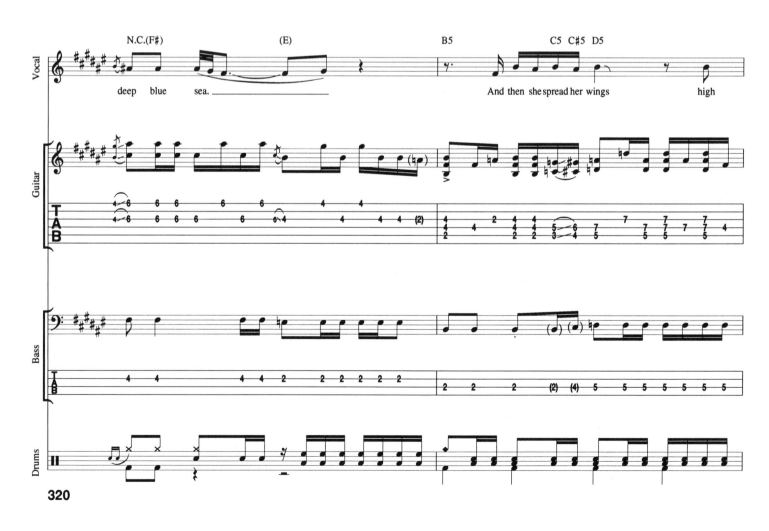

324

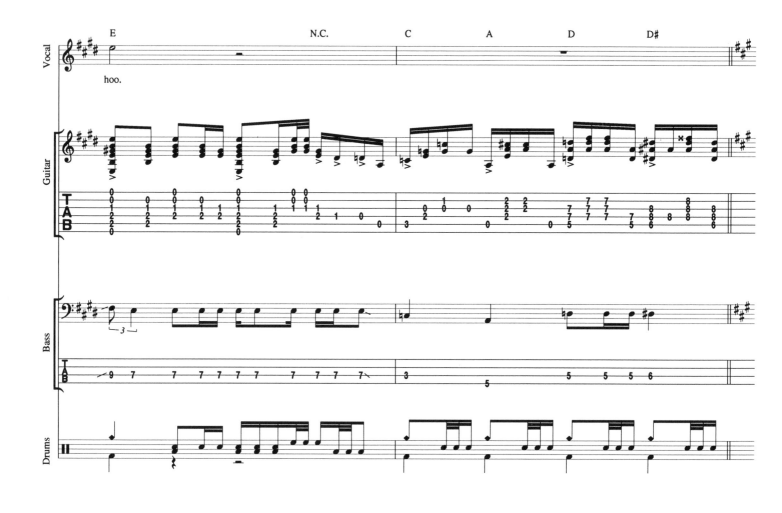

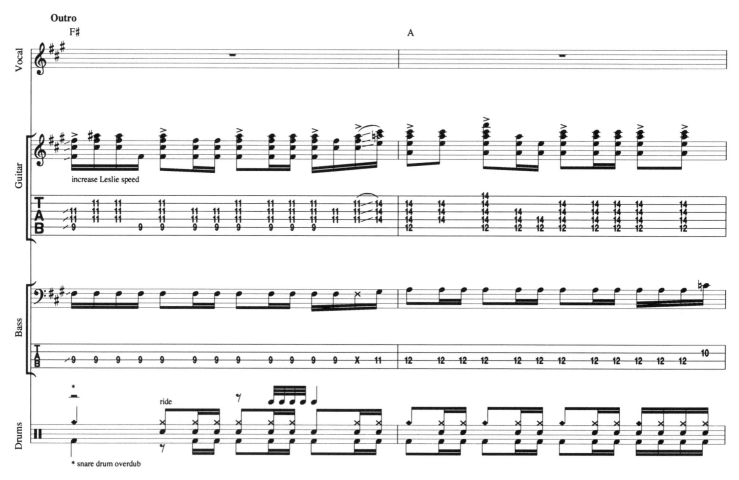

* floor tom overdub 1

* floor tom overdub 2, till end

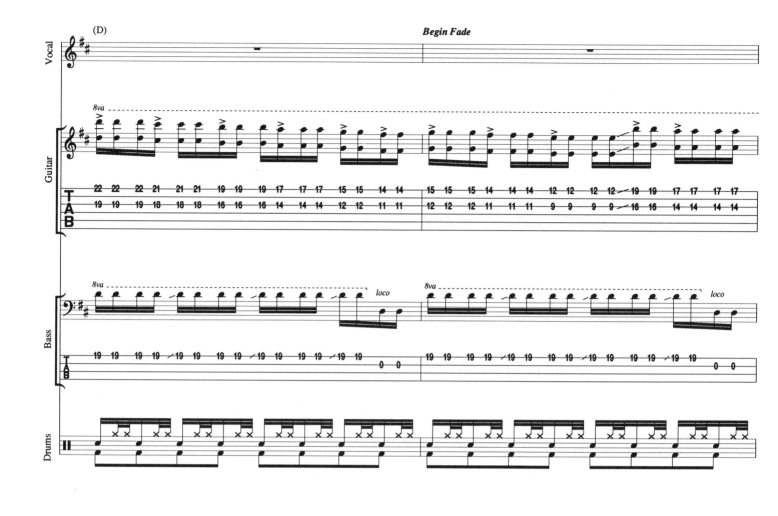

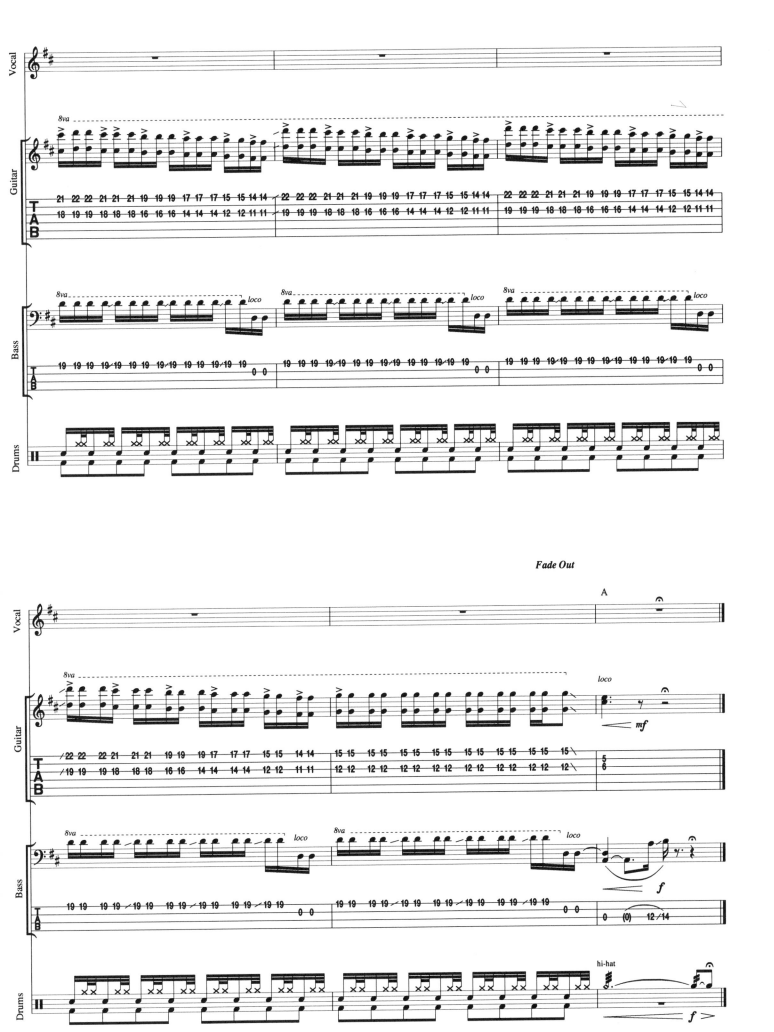

Fade Out

Dolly Dagger

Words and Music by Jimi Hendrix

A unison riff played by the guitars and bass opens this song, that was originally released in 1971 on the *Rainbow Bridge* album and re-released in 1997 on *First Rays of the New Rising Sun*. The use of unison riffs is also featured in the third and fourth, as well as the seventh through eleventh measures of the chorus.

The verse section is the essence of funk guitar. Tasty sixteenth-note strumming combined with more unison riffs become the key ingredients in the recipe that have made "Dolly Dagger" a favorite.

Copyright © 1971 by EXPERIENCE HENDRIX, L.L.C.
All Rights Controlled and Administered by EXPERIENCE HENDRIX, L.L.C.
All Rights Reserved

she drinks the blood from a jag - ged edge. ___ Aw, drink up, ba-by.
Woo. _____)

1. Been. rid - in' broom-sticks since

step a - side, _____ this chick's gon-na turn you to a block of ice. _____ Look out!

Mm. _____

2. Yeah,__ look at old __ burnt out Sup-er-man __ try'n' to shoot his dust __ on the sun.__

Verse

* Chord symbols reflect basic tonality.

* Probably meant A, ④ 7fr to stay in octaves w/ Gtr. 1

Outro

Dol - ly, ___ heav - y ma - ma,

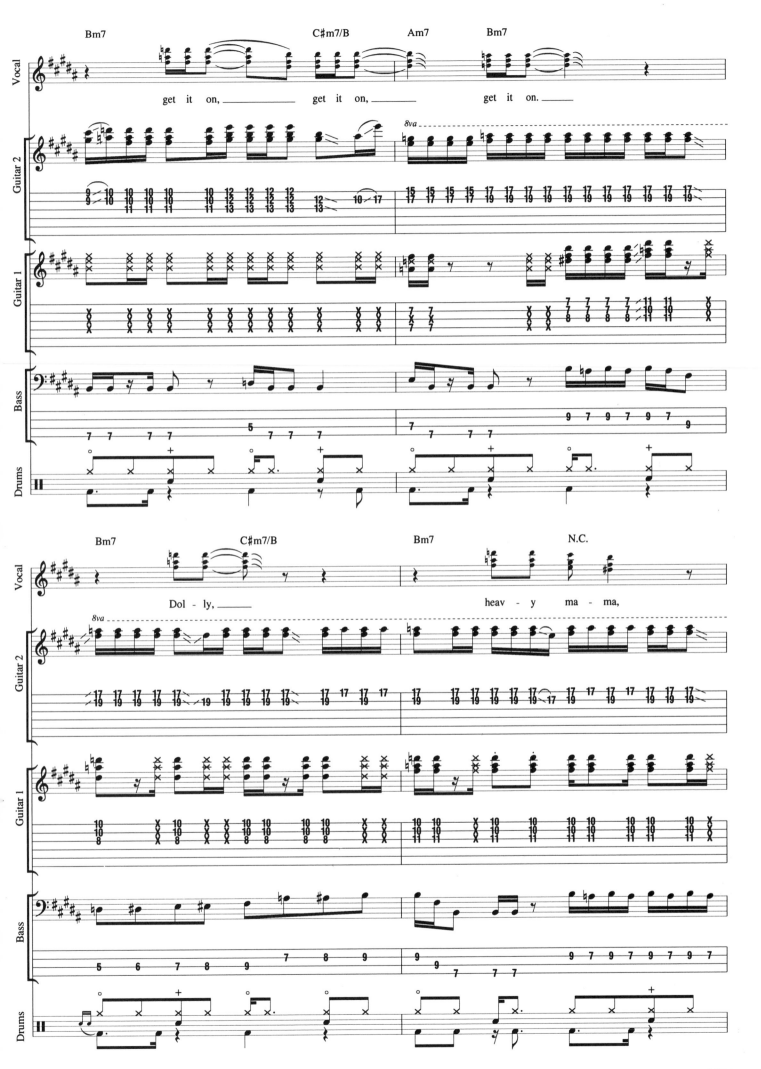

Star Spangled Banner

Adaptation by Jimi Hendrix

With a white Stratocaster blasting out unadulterated explosions of agony and ecstasy, long suede tassels flying everywhere as unprecedented, glorious sounds flowed from the pickups via masterfully manipulated vibrato bar, toggle switch, wah-wah, Fuzz Face, Univibe and wall of Marshall stacks, Jimi Hendrix closed the 1969 Woodstock festival with a mesmerizing performance that would forever change the face of rock music. His legendary rendition of "Star Spangled Banner" rode on pure inspiration, representing artistic expression taken to its zenith. That one moment, frozen in time, is equated with the peak of what the '60s aspired to be about, which was absolute freedom–the freedom to feel, think, dress and speak as one wished, and that maybe, just maybe, anything was possible. Jimi brought us all closer to that notion by making musical sounds on the guitar that, to this day, seem totally *impossible*.

Jimi liked to say that the reason he played "Star Spangled Banner" that day was because he used to have to sing it in school. Suffice to say, no vocal rendition would have sounded anything like this. Jimi plays the song's melody, which is based primarily on the E major scale (E, F♯, G♯, A, B, C♯, D♯) fairly straight for the first 22 measures, most of the time sticking to the song's original 3/4 time signature. Measures of 2/4 and 4/4 are inserted to best approximate Jimi's improvised phrasings. At measure 23, Jimi flies up the neck, bending a high E up one whole step to F♯, and then slowly releases the bend, simulating the whistling sound of a dropping bomb. In the next measure, the bomb explodes as a handful of open strings are smashed into, immediately dropped in pitch with the vibrato bar.

Starting at measure 25 [1:06], Jimi rips into a wild barrage of sounds that lasts for 29 seconds before the melody reappears [at 1:35]. This "sound segment," like the other improvised freakouts that occur during this piece, are written in "free time," with the phrasings approximated as clearly as possible. Similar blasts of feedback and vibrato bar abuse (including a very fast trill between the open G string and a fretted A♭ at the 13th fret [1:49], violently manipulated with the vibrato bar) carry the tune till the melody reappears at 2:21. Jimi inserts that old military favorite, "Taps," at 2:35, followed by the next four measures of the "Banner" melody [2:45-3:00]. During this section of the melody, Jimi quickly rocks the wah-wah pedal back and forth, creating the rhythmic effect of sixteenth-note triplets.

Following a generous dose of thick, vibrato-barred feedback on the D♯, Jimi, plays the melody's final theme [3:13-3:30] while masterfully manipulating the wah-wah pedal. He then blasts A, C and D major chords, followed by a crushing E5 chord, culminating this masterpiece.

Copyright © 1970 by EXPERIENCE HENDRIX, L.L.C.
All Rights Controlled and Administered by EXPERIENCE HENDRIX, L.L.C.
All Rights Reserved

362

Guitar Notation Legend

Guitar Music can be notated three different ways: on a *musical staff*, in *tablature*, and in *rhythm slashes*.

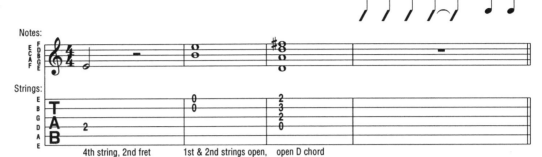

RHYTHM SLASHES are written above the staff. Strum chords in the rhythm indicated. Use the chord diagrams found at the top of the first page of the transcription for the appropriate chord voicings. Round noteheads indicate single notes.

THE MUSICAL STAFF shows pitches and rhythms and is divided by bar lines into measures. Pitches are named after the first seven letters of the alphabet.

TABLATURE graphically represents the guitar fingerboard. Each horizontal line represents a string, and each number represents a fret.

4th string, 2nd fret   1st & 2nd strings open, played together   open D chord

---

HALF-STEP BEND: Strike the note and bend up 1/2 step.

WHOLE-STEP BEND: Strike the note and bend up one step.

GRACE NOTE BEND: Strike the note and bend up as indicated. The first note does not take up any time.

SLIGHT (MICROTONE) BEND: Strike the note and bend up 1/4 step.

BEND AND RELEASE: Strike the note and bend up as indicated, then release back to the original note. Only the first note is struck.

PRE-BEND: Bend the note as indicated, then strike it.

VIBRATO: The string is vibrated by rapidly bending and releasing the note with the fretting hand.

WIDE VIBRATO: The pitch is varied to a greater degree by vibrating with the fretting hand.

HAMMER-ON: Strike the first (lower) note with one finger, then sound the higher note (on the same string) with another finger by fretting it without picking.

PULL-OFF: Place both fingers on the notes to be sounded. Strike the first note and without picking, pull the finger off to sound the second (lower) note.

LEGATO SLIDE: Strike the first note and then slide the same fret-hand finger up or down to the second note. The second note is not struck.

SHIFT SLIDE: Same as legato slide, except the second note is struck.

TRILL: Very rapidly alternate between the notes indicated by continuously hammering on and pulling off.

TAPPING: Hammer ("tap") the fret indicated with the pick-hand index or middle finger and pull off to the note fretted by the fret hand.

NATURAL HARMONIC: Strike the note while the fret-hand lightly touches the string directly over the fret indicated.

PINCH HARMONIC: The note is fretted normally and a harmonic is produced by adding the edge of the thumb or the tip of the index finger of the pick hand to the normal pick attack.

PICK SCRAPE: The edge of the pick is rubbed down (or up) the string, producing a scratchy sound.

MUFFLED STRINGS: A percussive sound is produced by laying the fret hand across the string(s) without depressing, and striking them with the pick hand.

PALM MUTING: The note is partially muted by the pick hand lightly touching the string(s) just before the bridge.

RAKE: Drag the pick across the strings indicated with a single motion.

TREMOLO PICKING: The note is picked as rapidly and continuously as possible.

VIBRATO BAR DIVE AND RETURN: The pitch of the note or chord is dropped a specified number of steps (in rhythm) then returned to the original pitch.

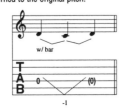

VIBRATO BAR SCOOP: Depress the bar just before striking the note, then quickly release the bar.

VIBRATO BAR DIP: Strike the note and then immediately drop a specified number of steps, then release back to the original pitch.

365

Bass Notation Legend

Bass music can be notated two different ways: on a *musical staff*, and in *tablature*.

THE MUSICAL STAFF shows pitches and rhythms and is divided by bar lines into measures. Pitches are named after the first seven letters of the alphabet.

TABLATURE graphically represents the bass fingerboard. Each horizontal line represents a string, and each number represents a fret.

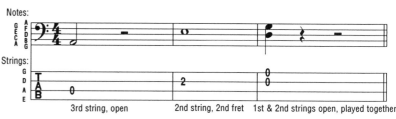

3rd string, open   2nd string, 2nd fret   1st & 2nd strings open, played together

HAMMER-ON: Strike the first (lower) note with one finger, then sound the higher note (on the same string) with another finger by fretting it without picking.

PULL-OFF: Place both fingers on the notes to be sounded. Strike the first note and without picking, pull the finger off to sound the second (lower) note.

LEGATO SLIDE: Strike the first note and then slide the same fret-hand finger up or down to the second note. The second note is not struck.

SHIFT SLIDE: Same as legato slide, except the second note is struck.

TRILL: Very rapidly alternate between the notes indicated by continuously hammering on and pulling off.

TREMOLO PICKING: The note is picked as rapidly and continuously as possible.

VIBRATO: The string is vibrated by rapidly bending and releasing the note with the fretting hand.

SHAKE: Using one finger, rapidly alternate between two notes on one string by sliding either a half-step above or below.

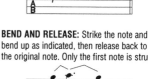

NATURAL HARMONIC: Strike the note while the fret hand lightly touches the string directly over the fret indicated.

MUFFLED STRINGS: A percussive sound is produced by laying the fret hand across the string(s) without depressing them and striking them with the pick hand.

BEND: Strike the note and bend up the interval shown.

BEND AND RELEASE: Strike the note and bend up as indicated, then release back to the original note. Only the first note is struck.

RIGHT-HAND TAP: Hammer ("tap") the fret indicated with the "pick-hand" index or middle finger and pull off to the note fretted by the fret hand.

LEFT-HAND TAP: Hammer ("tap") the fret indicated with the "fret-hand" index or middle finger.

SLAP: Strike ("slap") string with right-hand thumb.

POP: Snap ("pop") string with right-hand index or middle finger.

Additional Musical Definitions

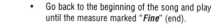

(accent) • Accentuate note (play it louder)

(accent) • Accentuate note with great intensity

(staccato) • Play the note short

⊓ • Downstroke

∨ • Upstroke

D.S. al Coda • Go back to the sign (𝄋), then play until the measure marked "***To Coda***," then skip to the section labelled "***Coda***."

D.C. al Fine • Go back to the beginning of the song and play until the measure marked "***Fine***" (end).

Bass Fig. • Label used to recall a recurring pattern.

Fill • Label used to identify a brief pattern which is to be inserted into the arrangement.

tacet • Instrument is silent (drops out).

  • Repeat measures between signs.

 • When a repeated section has different endings, play the first ending only the first time and the second ending only the second time.

NOTE: Tablature numbers in parentheses mean:
1. The note is being sustained over a system (note in standard notation is tied), or
2. The note is sustained, but a new articulation (such as a hammer-on, pull-off, slide or vibrato begins, or
3. The note is a barely audible "ghost" note (note in standard notation is also in parentheses).

Drum Notation Legend

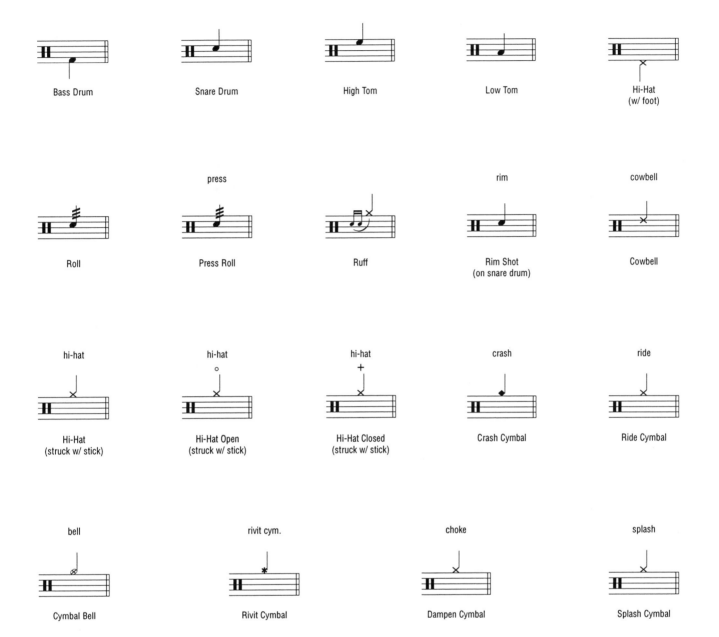

Study the master with these transcriptions and explorations of the techniques and tunes that made Hendrix a legend.

Guitar Recorded Versions folios feature complete transcriptions for guitar plus rare photos and extensive introductions. Easy Recorded Versions feature guitar transcriptions with the harder solos removed. Transcribed Scores feature note-for-note transcriptions in score format for *all* the instruments in each recording. All books include notes and tablature.

Are You Experienced

11 songs from the album including: Are You Experienced • Foxey Lady • Hey Joe • Manic Depression • Purple Haze • The Wind Cries Mary • and more.

00692930 Guitar Recorded Versions $19.95
00660097 Easy Recorded Versions $12.95
00672308 Transcribed Scores (17 songs)..... $29.95

Axis: Bold As Love

13 songs from the album, including: Bold As Love • Castles Made of Sand • Little Wing • Spanish Castle Magic • and more.

00692931 Guitar Recorded Versions $22.95
00660195 Easy Recorded Versions (12 songs) $12.95
00672345 Transcribed Scores $29.95

Band of Gypsys

Contains note-for-note transcriptions of: Who Knows • Machine Gun • Changes • Power to Love • Message of Love • We Gotta Live Together. Includes introduction and playing tips.

00690304 Guitar Recorded Versions $19.95
00672313 Transcribed Scores $29.95

Electric Ladyland

16 songs from the album, including: All Along the Watchtower • Have You Ever Been (To Electric Ladyland) • Voodoo Child (Slight Return) • and more.

00692932 Guitar Recorded Versions $24.95
00672311 Transcribed Scores $29.95

First Rays of the New Rising Sun

Matching folio to the new release featuring 17 songs whose creation spans from March 1968 through to Jimi's final sessions in August 1970. Includes 24 pages of color photos and extensive notes on each song.

00690218   Guitar Recorded Versions $24.95

The Jimi Hendrix Concerts

A matching folio to all 12 songs on the live album with authoritative transcriptions for guitar, bass, and drums with detailed players' notes and photographs for each composition. Songs include: Fire • Red House • Are You Experienced? • Little Wing • Hey Joe • Foxy Lady • Wild Thing • and more.

00660192 Guitar Recorded Versions $24.95

Radio One

A matching folio to all 17 songs on the album of Jimi's live radio studio performance. Includes authoritative transcriptions for guitar, bass and drums with detailed players' notes and photographs for each composition. Songs include: Hear My Train a Comin' • Hound Dog • Fire • Purple Haze • Hey Joe • Foxy Lady • and more.

00660099 Guitar Recorded Versions $24.95

Woodstock

Relive Hendrix's Woodstock performance with these 11 guitar transcriptions plus an introduction and photos. Songs include: Red House • The Star Spangled Banner • Villanova Junction • and more.

00690017 Guitar Recorded Versions $24.95

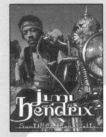

South Saturn Delta

Matching folio to the recent release of 15 tracks, including lost gems like "Tax Free," "Look Over Yonder," and "Pali Gap," as well as previously unreleased recordings like "Here He Comes (Lover Man)," "Message to the Universe" and "Midnight Lightning," and more.

00690280 Guitar Recorded Versions $24.95

Experience Hendrix – Book One Beginning Guitar Method

by Michael Johnson
This book/CD pack has been designed to guide you through a step-by-step process of learning music and guitar basics using the songs of Jimi Hendrix! It teaches guitar basics, music basics, music/guitar theory, scales, chords, transposing and progressions, basics of songs, blues, reading music and includes guidelines for practicing, tips on caring for your guitar, and much more. The accompanying CD includes actual Hendrix tracks to practice with, and on-line support for the method is provided by the Experience Hendrix website.

00695159 Book/CD Pack $14.95

FOR MORE INFORMATION, SEE YOUR LOCAL MUSIC DEALER, OR WRITE TO:

HAL•LEONARD® CORPORATION

7777 W. BLUEMOUND RD. P.O. BOX 13819 MILWAUKEE, WI 53213

Prices and availability subject to change without notice.

0898